SPECTRUM®
READERS

LEVEL 1

D0720354

WOW!
Big Animals

By Katharine Kenah

Carson-Dellosa
Publishing

SPECTRUM®

An imprint of Carson-Dellosa Publishing, LLC
P.O. Box 35665
Greensboro, NC 27425-5665

carsondellosa.com

Printed in the USA. All rights reserved.
ISBN 978-1-62399-134-0

01-002131120

Animals are all around you.
Some animals are
too small to see.
Some animals are big beasts!

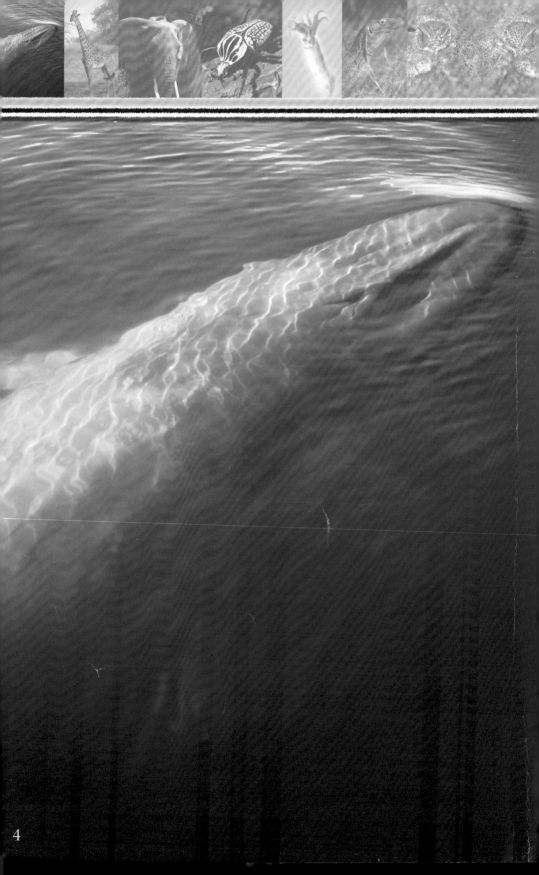

Blue Whale

The blue whale is the biggest
animal in the world.
It is as long as
three school buses.

Giraffe

The giraffe is the tallest
animal in the world.
It is about as tall as
a two-story house.

African Elephant

The African elephant is
the biggest animal on land.
It weighs as much as
two pickup trucks.

Goliath Beetle

The goliath beetle is one of the biggest bugs in the world. It is about as big as your hand.

Giant Squid

The giant squid is the biggest
animal with no backbone.
Its eyes are the size
of dinner plates.

Komodo Dragon

The Komodo dragon is
the biggest lizard in the world.
It is longer than
a picnic table.

Crocodile

The crocodile is the biggest reptile in the world.
It is longer than two bikes.

Ostrich

The ostrich is the biggest
bird in the world.
Its eggs are the size
of footballs.

Anaconda

The anaconda is the biggest
snake in the world.
It is about as long
as a garden hose.

Saint Bernard

The Saint Bernard is one of the biggest dogs in the world. It weighs as much as a full-grown man.

Siberian Tiger

The Siberian tiger is
the biggest cat in the world.
It is as long as two bathtubs.

Whale Shark

The whale shark is the biggest fish in the sea. Its mouth is as wide as a teacher's desk.

Stick Insect

The stick insect is the longest insect in the world. It is about as long as a ruler.

Albatross

The albatross is one
of the biggest seabirds.
Its spread wings are about
as wide as a two-lane road.

WOW! Big Animals
Comprehension Questions

1. What is the biggest animal in the world? How long is it?

2. How much does an African elephant weigh? Where do you think it might live?

3. Where do you think the giant squid lives?

4. Which do you think is longer: The world's biggest lizard or the world's biggest reptile?

5. What is an anaconda?

6. Do you think a Saint Bernard weighs more or less than you?

7. About how long is a stick insect?

8. What do you think is the smallest animal in this book?